TABLE OF CONTENTS

Introduction

Starting your own business is not an easy task! It doesn't matter if it is a large or small business; there will always be roadblocks and challenges to be faced along the way. Brick and mortar businesses have been around for a long time and have developed well-established procedures for others to follow. If you are opening a physical restaurant, there's a good chance you can easily find someone to help you navigate through your journey.

But what if your business is mobile and is set to operate in multiple areas, cities, counties, and regions? In this case, there are fewer proven strategies and procedures to follow. The freedom to roam around with your business is littered with challenges... most of which are unique to almost every truck. Being in a new place each and every day can wear on almost any food truck owner. From health codes to inventory management to budgets, you've got to have a strong will to survive in this type of business.

From the viewpoint of an outsider, the food truck business appears to be a lot of fun! And this is what is typically perceived by onlookers and customers thinking about starting their food truck. What isn't necessarily visible on the surface is all the hard work that goes into getting the truck up and running, setting up a profitable menu, marketing, pricing, mechanical maintenance, adhering to regulations, staffing, and much more!

Running your own food truck business requires more than just a passion for preparing and serving great food! It takes a lot of research and planning before a single penny is spent for the purchase of an actual food truck. Composing a detailed business plan is essential in the early stages. Even with a sound business plan in place, don't be surprised if things get more expensive than you originally budgeted in the startup phase. That is a sentiment shared by many food truck owners.

In today's world, there is a new trend of street food connoisseurs invading the new hot spot, food truck, food festival, or that little mobile food court on the corner. Although food businesses are not a new concept for entrepreneurs and consumers, it is one of the preferred activities of young adults and 20 something-year-olds. This generation is increasing year over year, and will be, if it already isn't, the biggest age-pool of customers in the world population.

These food lovers are always on the hunt for the newest food and beverage mix, trendy hotspot, or that iconic favorite that they can tell everyone they know about. All food businesses, whether a brick & mortar location, mobile business, booth, etc. must be aware not only of what the trends are but also must be aware of the legislation regarding food safety. As a business owner, you are ultimately responsible for ensuring that the food you are serving is well received and safe.

Food truck businesses are increasing partly due to the economic fluctuations in the past several years. There is a sudden upsurge trend that has started off, with consumers seeking inexpensive meal options that can be served in short amount of time. Although in the beginning, this had a slight effect on food-based businesses that are brick and mortar based, restauranteurs were quick to add on food trucks as part of a new revenue stream.

From an entrepreneurial standpoint, food trucks, mobile food businesses, and booths/cart setups have lower overhead expenses than restaurants and can easily relocate to pursue new revenue streams if needed.

From a consumer perspective, there is something amazing about not having to commute to get good food when the food will now come to you at lesser cost. There are a variety of options for those who want to start a food business:

- Restaurant
- Full Service
- Quick Service
- Delivery
- Retail Location
- Shop

- Farmers Market

- Concessions

- Wholesale

- Boutiques

- Big Box Stores

But first, let us talk about the misconceptions of owning a business and the common mistakes aspiring entrepreneurs make before they even get their business off the ground.

These assumptions and mistakes are typically facts and suggestions everyone hears from their peers without really looking into what is being told. These suggestions lead to false assumptions about what having a business is like, what it will involve, and how much money can be made. Most of the assumptions an aspiring entrepreneur has are usually unrealistic. Having unrealistic assumptions about owning a business usually leads to wrong strategies for the business, which in turn creates uncontrollable problems, causing business failure.

CHAPTER 1

Who Stops at Food Carts?

....for the people eating at these carts, never appear to grow old. That is because people genuinely appreciate getting those special foods at the festival like southern style doughnuts or cinnamon almonds. These are special treats that the old and youthful alike can't leave behind when they land at a fair. Be that as it may, at that point you have the food trucks that are perched on ordinary streets, the ones that offer healthy foods to grown-ups searching for a snappy lunch on their way back to work. These trucks are excellent too because the food they offer is modest and quick. Numerous business people stop at food trucks each day and increasingly more people appear to pick this lunch alternative regularly.

If you need to start up your own business yet aren't sure what to get into, take a gander at these versatile kitchens. If you've generally longed for having your eatery, however, are frightened by the cost and duty required, then food trucks can be a venturing stone as they get you into the food-service industry for lower speculation and you can fabricate a name and notoriety for yourself and your product. At that point the progression to an out and out retail facade café can be more straightforward. Food trucks are moderately easy to begin and they're mainstream for new business owners as well as for the overall population also. Numerous food truck owners love running it and the fact that everybody around appreciate and patronize them for some excellent quality food, at reasonable costs and quick service. It's undoubtedly a win-win for everybody included. Be that as it may, in case you are as yet not persuaded there's still more to this story.

Food carts are unique. For people who live in enormous urban communities, they may turn out to be simply one more piece of the scene (even though that doesn't stop them from eating at them frequently). However, for people who aren't used to the vast city the idea of eating at a food cart is fascinating, new and unique. These people couldn't care less that the food you are serving isn't gourmet (in spite of the fact that you'd be astonished at the assortment of food types accessible from portable food vendors nowadays), all they need is to give it a shot since that is the thing that 'enormous city people' do. So, there's dependably another person willing to attempt what you bring to the table.

The Freedom to Move

Another great thing about food carts as a business is that they can be on the move. With a physical customer facing facade, you are tied down to that place. If you pick a place and it ends up being dead space where nobody goes, then you are doomed, thanks to it. A food cart allows you to move around and go any place you please (inside the guidelines, obviously!). So, if one day you are on a street corner that doesn't have much business, the following day you can move elsewhere. If you start on one street; however, it starts to get exhausting you can move along from that point too. You can even be a portable street cart that moves around throughout the day.

The beginning is easy with the right data, making a profit is altogether attainable if you've set yourself upright and you never need to stress over running out of people to serve or getting exhausted with the view. Since there's less hazard in a portable food vending business than numerous different types of private ventures, you and your new food cart can be set for a great start right from the earliest starting point.

CHAPTER 2

What Is Cheaper to Run, A Restaurant, or A Food Truck?

W hich of the two are more environmentally friendly or economical to operate or is there no conclusive answer? At present, numerous people may rapidly accept that food trucks are the more regrettable of the two evils of the national focus on how naturally economical practices tie to methods of transportation.

However, sustainability is something that becomes an integral factor at whatever point a light is turned on, plastic is tossed into the trash, dishes are washed, and so forth. Environmentally friendly (or destructive) practices don't begin and stop with the key in the ignition; however, they rather occur during and after every single working hour of a business -- in a food trailer or in a customary physical café.

How about we take a look at the components that become possibly the most important factors during these business tasks.

The location: As you most likely are aware, catering trucks are mobile. They move all around and subsequently leave a smaller impression on where they've been. There's little framework, besides the business kitchen, that should be kept up. And then, there are eateries. Cafés have numerous huge areas that must be lit up, cleaned regularly, and temperature regulated. These physical elements exist constantly, not simply during working hours.

Energy Use: As referenced above, a conventional café's physical area makes the requirement for electricity and natural gas to keep up comfortable temperatures and to give light to eating clients. In the kitchens, cooking is commonly done with natural gas and frying pans and stoves are kept hot during the working hours. As per the 2003 Commercial Building Energy Consumption Survey, most eateries utilize 38.4kWh of electricity per square foot every year, which is roughly 77,000 kWh every year for a 2,000 sq. ft. eatery.

Food trucks likewise require a heat source for cooking, so they commonly use propane. During a year, a normal food trailer will utilize around 900 gallons of propane, in addition to fuel prerequisites for driving around. In spite of the fact that this fuel is generally diesel or gas, catering trucks may likewise utilize biodiesel or vegetable oil. Besides, an onboard generator addresses the electricity issue. While generators are normally more polluting than grid-provided power, food trailers demand less power and depend more on natural light.

Vehicle miles: Although restaurants can't pile on miles going to clients, their clients are most likely traveling to get to these customary eateries. A short outing by a food truck can frequently counterbalance various little excursions by clients that would have generally driven to an eatery.

Waste: For the waste component in the food business, it's a tie between food trucks and eateries. While some catering trucks are considered eco-friendly by utilizing corn-based plastic, bagasse, or reused paper takeout compartments, despite everything they're making squanders. Conversely, eateries can utilize reusable plates, cups, and utensils; be that as it may, take-out and fast-food eateries frequently depend vigorously on take-out containers that are made of Styrofoam and plastic.

Is the winner clear yet? From this subjective analysis, clearly, mobile food stands generally produce less hurtful ecological effects. It is completely conceivable that a few eateries will be more sustainable than other food trailers.

Keep in mind, as a food truck proprietor you should pay attention to your clients' interests. Your enthusiasm for ecological practices will hold steadfast followers and pull in new clients to your business.

Pros of Food Trucking

- Money! And loads of it. Regardless of whether you need two or three hundred dollars per week, several hundred a day, or a couple hundred per hour... these are for the most part realistic figures in mobile concessions.

- Freedom! You make your very own hours. Work 1 day a week or work 7 days every week. Take a multi-week excursion at whatever point you need. It's up to you. You are the chief. This can also be perilous. So, if you aren't spurred, this isn't for you. You will wind up with a costly residue collector in your carport.

- You can begin with next to zero cash.

- No nagging boss or corporate structure.

Cons of Food Trucking

- This is work, it is difficult to work and extended periods of time.

- Obtaining licenses.

- Learning and following the city and state guidelines.

- Obtaining insurance, license, and a commissary.

- Inventory and prep work.

- The daily tidying up.

- Working around extraordinary climate or finding shielded zones.

Drafting the Business Plan

After you and your partners have decided on what roles to play and how to split the profits, the next thing to do is to draft the business plan. This is the stage where the big idea will begin to take shape. We will go over some of the important points that you will need for your business plan and then we will take a look at an example of an actual business plan but first, why do you need one?

What is a business plan and why is it required?

Business plans are required if you are seeking third-party capital from banks, the small business administration, or other lenders.

Even if you are not required to put one together to get such financing, the initial preparation and planning are critical to the success of your business and will likely help you avoid costly mistakes.

If partners are involved the business plan is even more important to ensure the alignment of vision, necessary to avoid later disputes that can threaten the survival of the business.

Points to Ponder in The Planning of Food Truck Business

Certain items unique to the food truck business should be included in your planning such as:

The Local Food Truck Marketplace

The Market Analysis portion of the business plan is one of the hardest to make since it takes a lot of objective data gathered from the research of both primary and secondary sources.

In this case, we are interested in opening up a food truck business. Some industry research and statistics may be called for but the best research will be familiarizing yourself with local brands. This means internet research on the kinds of food trucks in your area (to help with differentiation and branding).
It also makes sense to look for "food truck lots." Many cities have parking lots that are leased or used by a collection of trucks for the business lunch crowd. In many cases, food trucks are parked here permanently and have a predictability that many food truck businesses lack. This may be the safest place to start your new business because you will have documented foot traffic, predictable food costs, and relatively consistent sales, which are rare in the industry. The potential downside here is that your brand will need to be materially different than the offerings from the other trucks.

It also makes sense to research the annual local fairs, festivals, and events within 50 miles of your home base. This information is easy to find online and organizers are often very happy to give you attendance and exhibitor cost information because they want you there. This information can help you project costs and illustrate to potential investors where you plan to seek revenue in building your business.

Understanding the Competition

Once you have worked through the local market, you will need to isolate the trucks that are either in direct or indirect competition with the truck you have conceived. *Direct competition* would be a substantially similar menu offering to the one you have in mind and you would want to make sure that you are not setting yourself up to compete with an established brand in a narrow marketplace. *Indirect competition* would be some overlap in the menu but sufficient difference in offerings that clients would conceivably be attracted to both businesses independently, were they to be at the same venue. Adjusting your menu may be a way to reduce concerns that arise from the direct and indirect competition.

Differentiation in the brand and product offering is critical to food truck success and should be a huge part of your business plan. This doesn't mean you shouldn't start a food truck that is similar to another in the area but it does mean that you should do so only after working out how you plan to compete with that truck. The strategy for success, however, is often more complicated than that.

Will you offer better quality food, a larger menu, longer service hours, or a better price? Perhaps some combination of these?

Business Strategy

In planning the business strategy, there are four basic business approaches that you can use to increase the likelihood of success for your business. These are cost leadership, differentiation, location, and hybrid.

Cost Leadership Strategy

This is very often the first strategy a new business seeks and it can be a devastatingly bad one. Frankly, it should only be considered in a rare set of circumstances. Specifically, this should only be considered for a very generic food offering in a high traffic environment. For example, if you are selling hot dogs, hamburgers, or fries at a state fair and can move tremendous volume, reasonable profit is still possible. To compete with this strategy, extra research is required to get the lowest possible food cost at a quality you can live with. Do not think that you will build a repeat following simply by being cheap. In fact, if not careful, you may send the message that your food is lower quality or less desirable to attract clients at a low cost.

Differentiation Strategy

The next strategy and one which more often makes sense is differentiation. As the name implies, the differentiation strategy would position your food truck in such a way that only you sell unique food products. Whether they are secret family recipes, hard to find food products, or creative dishes, these products set you apart because they cannot be offered by others. Quality is critical in the differentiation strategy but if the food is great and hard to find, your brand can achieve margins that are much more generous, leading to higher profits with lower sales and effort. This not only impacts the overall value of your business; it means a higher return on investment across the board.

Location Strategy

This can be a very effective strategy, especially at the start of the food truck for ensuring a solid, even loyal customer base. An example of this can be found with a truck owner we know in Los Angeles. He learned that a local clothing manufacturer had hundreds of employees, many of whom did not drive cars. He asked the owner of the company if he could serve breakfast and lunch to those employees and remit a small percentage of profits to the company for the right to set up there. The truck took off and is now permanently located there, with another truck purchased in a matter of a few months to grow the business. If you are aware of an area that is underserved by local restaurants or loaded with employees who cannot conveniently leave for lunch, this strategy can be very effective.

Hybrid Strategy

This strategy uses some combination of the above approaches to maximize the success of the truck. For example, we know of trucks that are in a particular place every Monday and another on Tuesday, etc. The scarcity created for customers when they know if they want that item for lunch, they have to get it on a certain day can increase brand loyalty. This approach would combine both location and differentiation while getting the extra benefit of spreading awareness of the brand. Others might have a different menu offering for festivals or particularly high traffic events to take advantage of cost leverage strategy while maintaining differentiation through a select offering of exclusive popular dishes.

Food Pricing

One of the hardest and perhaps most important parts of putting together a business plan is to decide on the pricing of the product. In the case of food trucks, there are methods and strategies on how to properly price your dishes so that they can appeal to your target market and also get to a good profit. Pricing should be based on the cost of the raw materials that were used to make the dish.

Typically, most food establishments would set their pricing at between 35 to 45 percent markup of the dish's cost, which would include the food and the plate, fork, garnishes, etc. So, let's say that you are serving a dish with ingredients that reach up to a total of $5. You may make it have a selling price of $7.25. You can experiment with price. Exclusivity can drive costs up. For example, baseball stadiums can often charge $6 for a $2 hot dog, because they have exclusivity. Your lunch crowd weekday guests are going to be much more sensitive to price than attendees at a festival, where there is an expectation that prices will be higher on food. If you price your items too inexpensively, you may quickly learn that the message you send customers is that the food isn't very good. Experiment and you will find a comfortable range for each menu item.

If you are surrounded by other trucks, take the time to walk the grounds and get a sense of their offerings and prices. You don't want to charge $4 for a bottle of water when all others are charging $2.

Another important consideration in pricing your items is labor, both in preparation in the kitchen and at the time of service from the truck. If a particular item is more labor-intensive than others on your menu, you may reasonably adjust the price to reflect that. Failure to consider that can lead to a lack of profits that demotivates the owner and sabotages the chances of success for the truck.

Use of Strategic Partnerships

Strategic partnerships should also be considered in the planning of the business. There is an exceptionally successful lobster roll brand that relies on a family fishing connection to provide an inexpensive product, that can be marked up for a very nice margin. This is an example of a supplier strategic partnership that can provide a competitive advantage, which makes the business more attractive to financing and improves chances of success. Other examples of strategic partnerships might be favorable lease rates or exclusivity offered by a business owner or festival organizer, with whom you share a small piece of the profit. It is worth your time to consider who you know and how to leverage those relationships for competitive advantage.

Similarly, even if you don't have a supplier connection, you should spend a substantial amount of time interviewing and sampling food vendors to negotiate price, ensure product quality and keep your hard costs as low as possible. Your efforts in doing so should be documented in your business plan, to show your preparation for success, to those who may invest in your business.

As you become more established and work with various events, it is a good idea to keep up the relationships you had with organizers of previous events that you went to. Many organizers are in this business. They can give you advanced notice and great opportunities for good locations and events.

It also really pays to have partners who are in the media. Whether you donate to a cause that will be celebrated by the media or offer a strange food offering that is newsworthy, this kind of attention can make your brand explode. Many food trucks offer food challenges such as an 8-pound burrito that is free if it can be finished by two eaters in less than an hour. Not much exposure from cost standpoint but an interesting story and often news outlets love these angles of human interest to fill into the gaps on slow news days.

CHAPTER 4

Financial Planning

What Numbers Should I Know?

"Know your numbers!" is a classic and overused phrase. However, it's vital to know your numbers—don't let the knowledge of them get away from you. Much stress and frustration can stem from the guessing game that ends up being played when you don't know your numbers.

You need to know how much money is coming in and going out every day, week, month, and year to know whether what you are doing is working. Knowing as much data as possible about your business will help take that guessing game off your plate and lighten the stress that comes with it.

The guessing game hurts you, your team, your business, and your customers. Once you know the basic numbers, you can start to dive in deeper. Then you can begin creating what I call "NextGen Numbers."

Later in this pin, I have included an extensive list of definitions and formulas on how to figure out those numbers.

Time to go beyond just knowing your numbers. Let's put them to work!

If you have your numbers in a program, it should be easy to break them down so you can see month-over-month and yearly trends. Utilizing these trends will help you get out of the guessing game and into making educated decisions based on the cold hard numbers, not what you feel.

Too often, people fall back into going with their gut feelings and what they knew to be true at one point in time. Things are changing every single day—in life and in business. It's imperative that you stay on top of the mounting trends in your business to avoid any blindside hits.

You can use the data you've collected to make investing in your business a lot simpler because you will know and not be guessing. Expanding and contracting areas of focus for your business will be leaps and bounds easier when you have the data laid out in front of you.

When was the last time you set sales goals for your business? You've heard that question before, I'm sure but I want you to take it one step further. Instead of just stating that you want to hit X sales goals for a period, track it and give periodic updates to your team based on the data available. That way your team can stay on task and on track to meet those goals. Tracking will also enable conversation on how to meet those goals. Without those conversations, you aren't giving your team a clear path to success, which is a quick way to wind up having unmet expectations and all-around disappointment.

Try to keep your goals obtainable and reasonable so you can use them as a springboard of encouragement for you and your team. Small wins are wins. You don't have to swing for the fences for a home run every time you go to set goals. Increases and decreases of 5 to 10 percent over specific periods of time should be reasonable. Setting such reasonable goals will also help with combating big downturns if you land the business that is a one-and-done deal. Next, we can move on to creating your own NextGen Numbers.

How Can I Create NextGen Numbers?

NextGen Numbers can be set for every position in your business and are different in every industry. They will help you track inefficiencies, which will save you money and add profit to your bottom line.

One example of a NextGen Number I created and used was to track the accuracy of our stock pickers in our central warehouse. Every day, hundreds of parts were picked off our central warehouse shelves to be sent to our satellite stores for stock and specific orders. We used a scanner and barcode system to create orders for the satellite stores that in theory should have been 100 percent accurate. As we quickly found out, that was far from the case.

Some members of our warehouse team were much more accurate in their scanning than others. The day after the inventory was sent, we would receive the corrections back. From there, I kept a running tally in a spreadsheet that gave team members a percentage score on their accuracy individually and as a whole. Based on this data, we determined we were able to lower our percentage of shipping errors out of our warehouse.

When it comes to figuring out what to track to base your NextGen Numbers on, you have to look at what data you have available to you. What data can you extract from the daily process you already have going on in your business? Once you decide what to track, you just need to keep a record of it in a spreadsheet. It doesn't need to be a super-complex spreadsheet but gather as many data points as possible to help you build an average and, most importantly, an expectation. Once you have that baseline of numbers, you can start to build an expectation and build predictions for how changes in your current process will affect the numbers. The results will most likely surprise you!

Once you have your basic numbers tracked and have goals built around them, you will be able to start finding and tracking these NextGen Numbers to start the process of building your business into a well-oiled machine.

Here's an outline of the basic numbers you should know to make educated decisions and help build your NextGen Numbers.

Expenses
Money spent in order to generate revenue.
Expense Target
The projected goal of the total expenses incurred during a specified time period.

Revenue
Income generated from sales.
Revenue Target
The projected goal of the total revenue during a specified time period.
Cost of Goods Sold
Cost of obtaining materials and creating the finished goods that are sold.
Formula: Beginning Merchandise Inventory + Net Purchases of Merchandise – Ending Merchandise Inventory

Profit
The surplus of money after total costs are deducted from total revenue.
Formula: (Revenue – Cost) / Revenue x 100
Profit Margin
Percentage of profit left after taxes.
Formula: After-Tax Profit x 100 / Cost of Sales
Net Profit
Total earned or lost in a specified time period. Formula: Total Expenses – Total Revenue

Gross Profit
Difference between revenue and cost of goods. Formula: Revenue – Total Expenses

Debt
Obligation to pay money.
Accounts Receivable
Amount of sales not yet paid for by customers.

Accounts Payable
Unpaid bills.

Return on Investment (ROI)
A percentage that compares profitability or efficiency of investments.
Formula: (Net Profit / Total Investment) x 100

Stock Turnover
The number of times inventory is replenished during a specific period.
Formula: Cost of Sales / Average Inventory

Sales
While it can be talked about as revenue, you should also know the number of units sold and the average number of transactions in a given period.
Sales Closing Rate
Percentage of prospects who become paying customers.
Formula: (Number of Successful Sales / Number of Leads) x 100

Average Time to Collect
The average amount of time it takes to collect your accounts receivables.

Salaries
The amount you are paying your team members in specific roles.
Cost of Customer Acquisition
Amount of expenses in marketing to acquire one customer.
Formula: Marketing Expenses / Number of Customers Acquired

How Do I Increase My Profit?

Now that you have gone through all of your numbers and even created new numbers to help, we can look at balancing your sales mix and examining ways to plus-up your current offer.

First, look at what percentage is coming from high-profit margin versus low-profit margin sales.
Now, take a look at how much you are spending on high-profit margin sales versus low-profit margin sales. This comparison will help you gauge how you can better spend your money and create a game plan for how you are

going to inject more high-profit margin sales into your mix. Allocating money for specific items in proportion to your overall budget will give insight into where to spend your capital to gain best outcomes.

Getting your mix right can include branching out into bringing more product lines together. You need to be careful, though, that you are not spending too much of your budget on betting whether a new product will take off with your customers. Identifying great add-on sale items that come with high-profit margins is the key to bolstering your overall profit margin. Don't be scared to try something new but make sure you educate your team on the benefits of selling the new products. If you have their support and they are educated, you are increasing your new products' potential success.

It's always easier to sell to existing customers than to find new ones. Getting feedback from your customers on what they would like to get from your business is always helpful for making more informed decisions. You can achieve that feedback in many different ways from just straight out asking the right questions to giving out surveys. You will most likely get opinions from the happiest or unhappiest people, so you will need to set up the survey to give you an average response.

A very crucial part of the business plan would be the break-even analysis as well as the profit forecast. These two calculations will give you an insight into how you must run your business in the first few months of operations and give comfort to financers as to your ability to repay the debt. While we are on that subject, don't try to convince a financer to loan you money on a truck that is in poor condition. Either find something new or in excellent condition or get a quote to put the truck in top condition. Do not expect a bank or finance company to lend its money on a bad truck and don't even think about doing that yourself. This is not a place to shortcut.

Let's take a look at how to compute for the break-even points first.

BEP or break-even point, in the context of a food truck operation, should be thought of in terms of:
P which symbolizes the price of each dish;
X which symbolizes the number of units per dish served.
V which symbolizes the variable cost per unit. Variable costs consist of costs that contribute directly to the forming of each unit of products (e.g.

ingredients to make the food, gas used for cooking). Variable costs are not standard and vary depending on the usage.

FC symbolizes the fixed costs that are incurred per month. Fixed costs are standard costs that you have to pay whether or not you make any money or not (e.g. electricity bill, phone bill, web server costs).

Now that we have the variables defined, let's talk about how to use them in a formula to solve for break-even points.

First, you can look for the BEP in units so you know how much food you should sell to reach the break-even point for the first year of operations. The BEP in units can be solved like this:

BEP X = FC/V-P

This is X (number of units to BEP) is equal to FC (fixed costs) divided by V (variable costs) minus P (unit price per dish).

Once you have the BEP number of units, you can now determine your BEP price. You simply multiply the price per unit and the BEP number of units to get your BEP price.

It is formulated as follows:

BEP Price = X (BEP X)

Now, this formulation is just assuming that you have one product in your store. However, since you have a food truck, you will most likely have a lot of dishes on your menu (including drinks and add-ons).

With this in mind, the more appropriate formulation to use would be to get the weighted averages for selling price and variable costs. After you get these two, you can plot them into your formula.

To get the weighted average, you can use this formula:

(Selling price of product 1 × Sales percentage of product 1) + (Selling price of product 2 × Sales percentage of product 2) + (Selling price of product 3 × Sales percentage of product 3) + (Selling price of product 4 × Sales percentage of product 4)........

To get the Sales percentage of the product, you have to decide on a ranking of the products to determine which will sell the most to which would sell the least. The total percentage of all the products will equal 100%, so you have to split the 100% to all these products.

Once you've computed the weighted average of all your dishes, then you also compute the weighted average for variable costs as shown below:

(Variable expenses of product 1 × Sales percentage of product 1) +
(Variable expenses of product 2 × Variable expenses of product 2) +
(Variable expenses of product 3 × Sales percentage of product 3) +
(Variable expenses of product 4 × Sales percentage of product 4) ....

After getting your weighted averages for variable costs and the selling prices, you can plot them into this formula:

BEP X = FC/ Weighted Average V - Weighted Average P

To better understand how to do this, we'll make use of a case scenario as an example.

Let's say you want to open up a burger food truck called Billy's Burger Stop wherein you will sell different kinds of burgers along with some fries and drinks.

At the start of the business, Billy's wants to introduce 3 burgers, 1 kind of fries, and lemonade.

Billy's will be selling Angus Burgers at $8,

Veggie Burgers at $7,

and Bacon Burgers at $8.

Billy's would also be selling fries at $4

And lemonade at $2.

Variable expenses would include $3 for Angus Burger,

$2.5 for Veggie Burgers,

$3 for Bacon Burgers,

fries at $1.50

and lemonade at 50c.

Billy's decided that the Angus Burger will have an SPP (sales percentage of product) of 30%,

Veggie Burgers 20%,

Bacon Burgers 20%,

fries at 10%

and lemonade at 20%.

To compute for the Break-even point, first, we compute for the weighted average of the selling price.

This would be (8x30%) + (7x20%) + (8x20%) + (4x10%) + (2x20%) = 5.6

After that, you get the weighted average of the variable cost which would be:

(3x30%) + (2.5x20%) + (3x20%) + (1.5x10%) + (0.5x20%) = 2.25

From there, we can plot the figures into the formula. Let's pack the FC at around $4,000 for everything including kitchen expenses, gas, rental, etc.
This will be 4,000/5.6-2.25 = 1045 units. This means that your truck would have to sell approximately 1,045 units to break-even.

Creating the Profit Forecast_

After you know how to compute for the Break-even Point, you can now go ahead and make your profit forecast. Your profit forecast is very important because it will help you determine what month you can reach break-even and when you will start profiting. You will also see all of your expenses to know how to do some pencil-pushing. Let's get started with the expenses.

Compiling All Expenses

Before you create the profit forecast, you must first list down all of your expenses. When you start your food truck business, you must think first about your overhead expenses which are the expenses that you use to get the business going. These would include the cost to get the truck, the advertising wrap for the truck, and the food inventory for the first six months. We have included a food cost projection tool, that allows for accurate planning on a per dish basis.

For your truck, you may choose to either rent or buy one. If you are renting a food truck, you will be paying a monthly fee for the usage while if you buy one, you will just pay everything outright, unless you get a note on the vehicle.

Be sure to think about what would be the kitchen expenses, particularly extra equipment that must be purchased or rent if using a prep kitchen.

You must also think about designing your truck and your truck advertising. Aside from that, you should also take into consideration the labor that you will use for your truck. Assistants and cooks may be needed depending on how big you want your business to be at the start.
If you plan to start lean, you may just have 2 or 3 prep and cooking staff.

Lastly, you must source for your ingredients and add that as expenses. These are the major expenses you have to think of.

Monthly Expense Forecasting Tool

	Month 1		
	Price	Quantity	Total Sales in Dollars
Unit Price	xxx	xxx	$ xxx
Less: Cost of Sales	xxx	xxx	xxx
Profit per Piece	xxx		xxx
Security Deposit and Advanced Rental Expense			xxx
Truck Purchase/Rent			xxx
Kitchen Purchase/Rent			xxx
Marketing Expenses			xxx
Business License and Registration			xxx
Utility Expenses			xxx
Salaries Expenses			xxx
Truck Design Expense			xxx
Miscellaneous Expense			xxx
Insurance			xxx
Total Expenses			XXX
Net Income/Loss			xxx

This forecasting table was designed to project costs on a per month basis.

It contains the price, the quantity, and the total price in dollars. The price heading would determine the unit price and the quantity heading would determine the estimated quantity that you can sell in the first month. The unit price multiplied by the estimated quantity will equal total sales in dollars.
You will also have the unit price row heading along with the cost of sales. To get the profit per piece, you have to subtract the cost of sales from the unit price. Under the total sales in dollars column heading, you will get the total gross profit for the month.

Right below that is the list of expenses. The list of expenses is to be totaled in order to get the total expenses for the month. From there we subtract the total expenses from the gross profit and we get the net income/net loss for the month. If the total profit exceeds total expenses, we have a net income, if it doesn't, then we have a net loss.

It is also through this table that you can determine how long it will take for you to reach your break-even point. Take note that this tool doesn't assume any additional or prior capital infusion.

Determining Capital Requirement

By determining the income forecast, you now can determine the required capital infusion for the business. Most people are conservative and would infuse capital to cover the first three to six months of expenses whether or not the business reaches the break-even point and count on the sales to increase. This gives you a window to make mistakes, learn what your real sales are and what items on your menu are driving business. It certainly makes sense to revisit financial projections, break-even, and profit/loss analysis every 30 days or so, in the beginning, to avoid purchasing food that you won't use or incurring unnecessary expenses.

Complete the projection tool above and plan for the number of months you will cover regardless of sales and base your capital requirement on the number reached by computing the total expenses for a period of time plus the cost of sales for the said period of time.

If you are borrowing capital to start the business, consider negotiating a delay in the first payment on the note for 90-120 days to allow you to reinvest in the business, so there is sufficient capital in the business for operations.

Accept Credit Cards Anywhere

If you run a food truck business or are in the process of getting it up and running, you are going to need to establish a way to accept payments from your customers. When the food truck industry was just starting to gain momentum, there weren't a lot of choices to choose from. Food truck owners mainly had to accept cash or checks and maybe use the old carbon paper-based credit card imprint machines. When you only accept cash, you limit the number of customers that can purchase from your truck.

Outside of the food truck industry, it's amazing that some restaurants still only accept cash! These days, not a lot of people carry around cash with them... and if they do, it's usually just a small amount. Most customers expect a business to be able to accept credit or debit card purchases. Imagine yourself in that same situation when you've ordered food or tried to buy something from a merchant that only accepted cash, only to find you had no cash on you. How would you feel when you are told that the transaction is cash only?

That is exactly how your customers will feel if they are not given the choice to use their credit card. But thanks to innovative entrepreneurs and their technology; mobile payment apps and portable card readers are now available for any type of business. You can now accept almost any type of credit card on the go. These mobile Point-of-Sale systems or POS are the cornerstone of how payments are made in the food truck industry today. If you have a smartphone or tablet, you can get up and running very quickly.

Mobile is all the rage when it comes to food trucks and how they process credit card transactions. The mobile solutions available on the market today provide new opportunities for new and existing food truck businesses. With the success of the current systems available, it's inevitable that more competitors will off their mobile payment solutions in the future. But no matter how many competitors enter the marketplace, you need to understand the basics of how all credit card systems work.

With so many choices on the market, choosing a mobile credit card payment system for your food truck business can be difficult. How do you make the right choice when they all have similar features and functionality? Do you make a decision based on the lowest fees or maybe the best customer feedback and reviews?

This book was not written to decide for you but rather to give you informative insight into the features, functionality, and details of mobile payment systems in general. This book also highlights the most popular units on the market so you can compare the features and operating procedures associated with each company. I want you to have the information you need to help you make the best choice for your business needs.

Every food truck business is different and each team has different dynamics when it comes to operations. Your expenses and expected volume of sales can play into which mobile payment system integrates into your business the best. No payment system is perfect and you probably won't find one with every feature you want.

CHAPTER 5

Expenses and Cash Flow

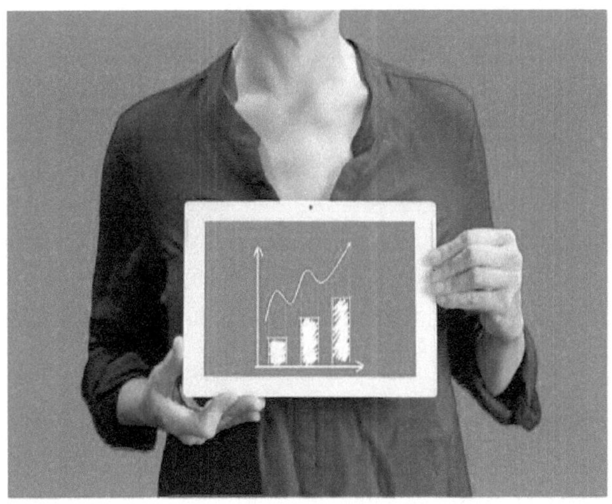

S tarting a business is expensive and you need to know how to cover your start-up costs before you can get your food truck idea off the drawing board and onto the streets. There's no doubt that menu planning and designing your truck are considered the "fun" aspects of this business. While it can also be fun running a food truck, just remember that it is still a business and should be treated like one. Looks can be deceiving but starting a food truck business is just like starting a regular restaurant except for the mobility and lower start-up costs. It's not a get rich quick business! It takes long hours and dedication to make it and survive in this industry.

To be successful, you need to watch your cash flow. This is achieved through proper pricing and smart supply purchases. Also, you need to keep a close eye on expenses. There are no set costs for starting a gourmet food truck business. Each food truck is unique and has different requirements. Start by making a list of all the expenses you can think of. Don't be surprised if your costs add up fast. You will need to calculate how much it costs to produce each dish. This is important because, in the beginning, you need to get a good idea of the amount of money needed to start and maintain your business. And don't forget legal, accounting, and other financial expenses.

Operating Expenses

Another part of the equation is operating expenses. Operating expenses are the ongoing costs that keep your business running. You can consider operating costs like recurring monthly payments. Breaking it down even further gives us fixed and variable expenses. Examples of fixed expenses can include commissaries, vehicle payments, vehicle rental, website hosting, and insurance. When it comes to variable expenses, ingredients, fuel, repairs, marketing, and special permits can fall into this category. It's important to be able to estimate your costs each month as accurately as possible. And you might need to anticipate a little extra for the unknown. Unexpected costs can come from last-minute events or vehicle repairs.

Keep in mind that it's going to take time for your business to become profitable. And it can be hard to watch the money fly out the door without any return on investment in the early months. The bigger your initial investment, the longer it will take to pay it back. One advantage of a food truck is that it has lower overhead costs. However, you will still need enough capital on-hand to be able to continue running for at least six months to a year in the beginning. Studies have shown that it often takes businesses at least two years to start showing profits. For most people, that is an eternity!

Managing Food Volume

You will need to effectively manage the volume of food. Here are the variables that help determine volume. Part of it is how much food you will buy and how much of it you are going to prepare. Then you will need to figure out how much you are going to sell. Calculating volume can be difficult. You can estimate your volume in the beginning to get a ballpark figure but only experience will make you better at estimating how much to buy and prepare.

The ongoing dilemma is figuring out how much food to bring to a service. This depends on how much you think you can sell. Often you won't know until you run out of food. And when you do run out of food, you won't know how much food you could've sold! This can be very frustrating.

The other challenge is that you only have a limited time to sell your food because you are not open all day like a traditional restaurant. You need to be able to serve foods quickly and increase volume. Another aspect that comes into play is pricing your menu correctly. There needs to be a balance in your pricing. If your prices are too high you won't sell much food. If your prices are too low, you won't make any money. On average, most food truck items are priced between $6 to $10 but some charge more.

Building Loyal Customers

To build a strong following for your truck, you need to have affordable prices. You can compare the prices of similar items from your competitors. Charging the right price is another skill that comes from experience. Your location plays a factor in determining what your customers will want to pay. Pricing in one city will be different than that in another city. Portion size helps determine your price also.

You need to identify what makes your food different from the competition. If you charge much higher than the competition, then you need to justify why it costs more.

Here are some reasons that you can charge more for your food than your competitors. You might be using organic ingredients or maybe you are including side dishes not offered by your competitors. Your portion size may be larger. Maybe you are using imported ingredients. Serving a gluten-free menu can also justify a higher price. The bottom line here is that if you are spending more than you are making, then adjustments will have to be made.

Adjustments you can make are lowering supply costs, getting bulk discounts for your ingredients, adjustments to employees, and staff size, you could join a co-op or you can improve your marketing strategies. When you've calculated your costs, determine how many items you need to sell just to break even.

The first year is going to be the most difficult to become profitable! The first year is also where most adjustments will be made. And of course, there'll be some factors that are out of your control like:

- Bad weather

- Event cancellations

- Health issues

- Vehicle breakdowns

It's all part of the business and every industry is faced with the same hurdles. Having lots of patience can go a long way to get you through the toughest parts of the start-up process.

CHAPTER 6

Marketing Strategies and Prices, Promotions, etc.

Offer Something for Free

Offering something small for free to each customer is a good way to ensure happy customers and to distinguish you from other trucks. It is also good for keeping people occupied. As the orders come piling in and the wait time becomes longer, giving people something small to snack on is a good way to keep them occupied until their food arrives. People can become impatient with the longer wait times but if they've already received something, they'll be more patient with you.

It all depends on what type of food you like to make but it is easy to give out free items that don't cost much. We've done homemade popcorn and homemade chips, as well as small desserts.

A small bag of popcorn to each person waiting won't cost you much and the benefits will be a happier and more tolerant customer. I have found this to be a good way to get a more friendly and loyal customer base, especially if you continually serve at a particular location.

Let the Order Line Be Longer Than the Pickup Line

This may sound a bit confusing so let me explain. If you have a large number of people waiting to order as well as people waiting for their food, it's a better idea to make the people looking to order wait than it is to let the people looking to pick up wait.

Once people have ordered, they're ready to take it and go; they get impatient very quickly. They know their order has been received and they're not thinking about all the other orders on the board, they just want theirs. People waiting to order, on the other hand, are only impatient because there are people in front of them in-line and so their impatience lies more with the people ahead of them than it does with you.

With a long list of orders on the board, things will get stressful in the truck pretty quickly. You will want to take orders but also be scrambling to get food orders out the window. However, from experience, it's better to hold off on taking more orders if there's a large number already on the board to concentrate on.

Let the people waiting to order know that you are busy clearing the board and will be with them shortly and focus on getting some of the orders out to waiting customers. That way you will keep people's wait times for their food down, which is generally more important than the line waiting to order.

Offer Items from Your Catering Menu

Though this book doesn't focus on the catering side of your business, serving food on the street is a good chance to promote it. A good way to do this is to offer 1 or 2 items from your catering menu. Assuming you have a catering menu, a good way to land catering gigs is to choose a couple of items from this menu for street service.

Now maybe your catering food is more tailored towards cocktail parties and smaller foods but that's fine. You can offer them as a side, give some out for free or change the item to make it more of a main dish and less of a smaller finger food type.

However, you do it, it's good to test out how people like the items you will be serving at your catering events. It will also be a good chance for people who may be planning a catering gig to get a taste of what they can expect if they book their gig with you.

If you make sure to promote it and make a note on your menu that the item is from your catering menu, it will let people know that you do cater and that this is the quality they can expect. So besides satisfying people's taste buds on the street, you will be subtly promoting your catering, which is where you can make very good money.

Assuming your food tastes great, this is a good way to attract people to your catering business and give people the idea of booking their gig with you.

Always Ask If They Would Like A Drink

This may sound painfully obvious but it's easy to forget. Especially if you are busy, you will be too focused on taking orders and getting food out the window and you may forget to ask each customer if they'd like a drink. In addition to putting drinks on the menu, it's a good idea to ask each person if they'd like to add a drink if they haven't already asked for one.

Every dollar counts and this is a good and effortless way to make a couple of extra bucks out of each order, which throughout a day of selling will start to add up. Again, you will want to price your food so that adding a drink can add to a number that goes with a bill. This won't be possible in all cases but try to keep it in mind.

For example, maybe your main item sells for $8. It isn't a stretch to ask 2 dollars for a can of Coke and most people won't think twice about handing you a 10-dollar bill. It's always a good idea as well to offer a discount if they include a drink with their meal or for a combo deal with a drink and a side.

Whatever you decide, be sure to ask every customer if they'd like to add a drink. A lot of people who wouldn't order one will end up getting one; you just have to put the idea in their head.

Advertise Your Menu on Social Media

This is important for several reasons. You will want your regular customers to know what you will be offering that day and hopefully, it's something they've had before and want to try again. It's also for people who haven't tried your truck. This is where a good menu is important, with great-sounding food. You will want those good descriptions to catch their eye and entice them to come and check your truck out.

I've found that it's rather boring just to write out what you are offering that day, especially if your main social media advertising is on hosts that are picture-based. This is where taking pictures of your food is important, as you can show them what you will be offering as well as describe it. This is where you will get people excited.

If they see what you are offering and it looks great, they'll be much more inclined to come to enjoy your food than if you were to just describe it. This can be done in many different posts, one for each item. That way you will give more people a chance to see your posts and they'll be able to see everything you are offering, hopefully enticing them to be excited about a number of your items.

In addition to pictures, add what each item consists of; just write the same description that's on your menu. The picture and description should be enough for people to want to come down and check it out. If your pictures look good and the description is intriguing, this shouldn't be difficult.

You should do this with your location: Throwing up a picture of what you will be serving and letting them know where and when they can enjoy it is a great way to combine these two. Do this when you know your location, throughout the week, and the day before and day of. That way you will build some anticipation and give more people a chance to see what they can hope to enjoy and how to get it.

Make Sure the Spot's Worth It

After spending all this time and money, you will want to make sure that, on average, you are making money. It's not as easy as it looks to turn a profit on a food truck. There are so many factors that are working against you, most of which you can't control. It may sound like I'm being negative but the truth is, losses can begin to pile up quickly and as such it's important from the get-go to recognize this and do what you can to mitigate these losses.

Whether it be bad weather, a poor customer turnout, or just pure bad luck, you will want to identify quickly if the spot you've chosen is worth it. Often, you will return to the same spot many weeks in a row. This makes sense, as it's not easy to find spots to park your truck, whether that's because of city regulations or because there just aren't that many good places to sell food. Whatever it is, you will want to decide quickly whether the spot you find yourself at is a spot you should continue to attend.

In a lot of instances, good spots can end up costing money before you even show up. This will depend on your city but sometimes your best bet is on private property and you will end up shelling over a reasonable amount of cash just for the right to sell there. This can be a minor expense if the spot is great but if it isn't, you could find yourself at a loss at the end of the day. Factoring in the fee to be there, food costs, truck costs, not to mention all the hours you put into making the food, you want to be turning a profit and if you are not, odds are you should find a new spot. Often, to focus on all the other factors that go into running a food truck business is easy but finding a good location, which is a big part of making money, is forgotten.

Be honest with yourself and if the spot sucks, don't keep showing up. Save that money you'd otherwise be wasting and find somewhere new where you can hope to establish a good customer base. It's better to go back to the drawing board than to keep throwing money at a venture that isn't profitable, especially at the early stages when you can't afford to waste money.

Proximity to like vendors: When participating in festival events, ask the event organizer to not place you next to food vendors that sell the same entrée items you are selling. Meaning if BBQ Pulled Pork is on your menu and your neighboring food vendor is selling BBQ Pulled Pork you are in direct competition with them. This can lead to confusion among prospective patrons and dwindle your sales.

These Pizza Truck vendors are in direct competition with each other

Best location: As you plan to participate in various events, some food vendor applications will allow you to select where you prefer to setup. As a general rule of thumb always select spots near the Beer Garden, Bathrooms, and ATMs. Why? Two words…**Foot Traffic**.

- Foot Traffic is your best friend when participating in festival events. Being close to the Beer Garden, Bathrooms and ATMs provide prospective vendors with the greatest exposure to patrons attending festival events.

Electrical power and water: The essentials of operating your food truck at festival events are water and electrical power. Electricity is required to operate your refrigeration equipment and water is required to wash your hands and dishes. Keep the following things in your hip pocket as you prepare:

- Bring an extension cord long enough to reach the power supply receptacle, a 50ft cord is sufficient.

- If you are unable to have a direct water connection from the event water source, bring a 5-gallon water jug to refill your freshwater tanks.

- Know how to reset the electrical breaker in case the power source gets overloaded with multiple electrical connections from other vendors.

Note the three hoses connected to the water spigot, two connections are directly connected to a food truck vendor's water source, the single-detached hose is for refilling water buckets.

Include a portable non-potable water container for collecting wastewater and a potable water container for clean water in your equipment inventory.

- Not all electrical and water source connections are the same, be prepared with various electrical adapters and water hoses in case the event organizer is unable to accommodate your connection needs.

Generator "Don't be that guy": There may be times when electricity is not available at the festival event due to logistics and the use of a generator is required. As a courtesy, always position your generator at least 25 feet away and behind your food truck or trailer. Generators produce a lot of noise. The noise produced by generators will disrupt customer interaction and make it difficult to hear patrons place their orders.

- Don't be that rude food vendor with a loud generator that disrupts fellow food vendors taking orders from customers.

Amperage; know what your equipment pulls: When filling in food vendor applications you will note a section reserved for amperage requirements. Typically, 20 AMPS or 30 AMPS is the norm. This is assessed by adding the total amperage of the electrical output of equipment installed on your food truck or trailer. Look at the specification label of your equipment to determine the amperage. When you identify the amperage for each electrical item used, the collective sum will be the total amperage you will include on your vendor application.

Finally, understand the appropriate electrical cords capable of carrying the correct electrical load for your food truck or trailer. Most <u>food trucks</u> operate on a 220 Volt 4-Prong connection and most <u>food trailers</u> operate on a 120 Volt 3-Prong connection.

Examples of various power plugs.

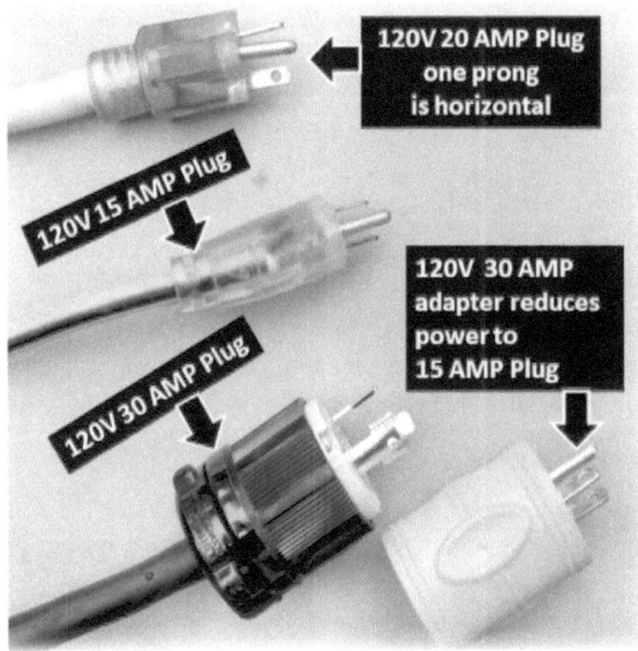

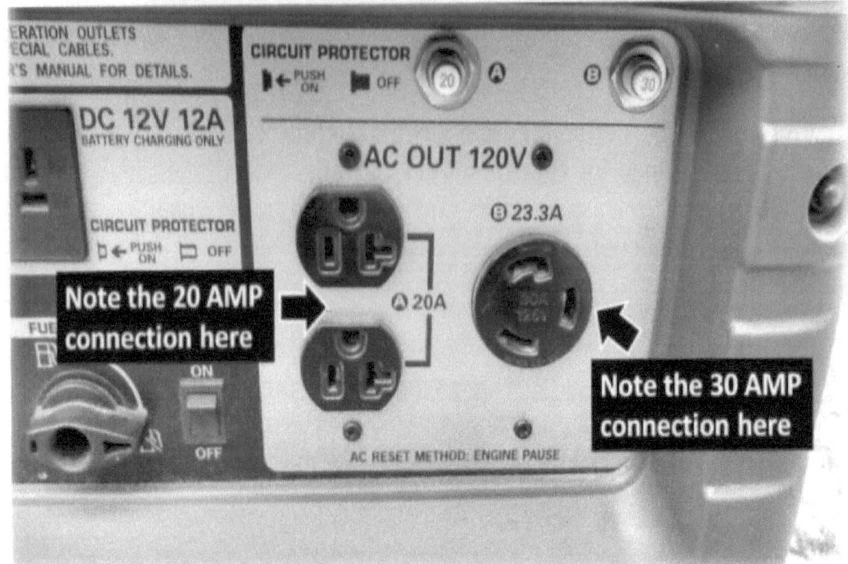

Electrical input connections for a Honda Generator

Food Truck Parking During Business Hours

Since space in larger cities is at such a premium, the rules for using said space are typically regulated more rigidly than they would be in a less populated city.

After you've scouted your food truck's prime spot, make sure you check with all local authorities what kind of permits and licenses you need to operate but also what's needed to keep it parked. Needs a special lease for space? What are the terms and conditions of the contract and are they transferable?

Food Truck Parking During Off Hours

When you've closed up the truck for the day, where are you parking it? When you live in the suburbs, you may have your driveway, where you can park the nighttime food truck. That's perfect because you don't have any additional costs. If you are not so lucky, you may need to hire or rent a space during non-business hours to park your food truck and that may add up to a few hundred dollars a month.

Event Parking

We will park this one right here because activities involving food trucks would normally cost you some money. Finding a prime location for your daily operations is critical to your restaurant's success on wheels but so is your involvement in food truck events–or events that feature a food truck aspect such as the Belmont Stakes Racing Festival Food Truck Village. Your attendance at these kinds of activities would typically cost only $200-$1000 to participate and the organizers may like a portion of your profits as well. Before committing, ensure you read the fine print.

Tools of Trade: Web Site, Cards, Stationery

So Much Digital Media, So Little Time

Once you have your first few events under your belt, it's time to make your business truly professional. You could have business cards and stationery made up before your first event but as I have suggested over and over, you are likely to change some things about your stand after you start doing events.

Preprinted stationery is so last century. Much more common now is to use a template in a word processing application for your letterhead. Business cards are incredibly easy to design and have printed these days.

A web site is another matter. To my way of thinking, every business ought to have a web site. I've been told my way of thinking is biased because I'm a "computer guy." That may be true and I enjoy designing my web pages, posting photos and videos from events to my "Pictures" pages, and maintaining an online calendar of my event bookings. But even if you have no computer skills at all, having a website for your business is incredibly easy.

You don't need any of the advanced code-writing used by sites with online ordering, logins, databases, or java script. A vendor web page only needs a few pictures and text. Your nineteen-year-old niece or nephew could probably do it for you. Your website should have a brief description of your business, a menu, or product guide, and how to contact you. This could all be on one page. For the more ambitious, the site could include a calendar page, pictures page, travel blog, cooking or crafting tips, or any other fun topic you might want to share.

The cost of having your own web site has dropped amazingly over the years. In the early days of the Internet, web site hosting and domain name registration could cost hundreds of dollars a month. Now those services can be found for under ten bucks a month. There are even services that will host your site free. The drawback is, since they have to make their money somehow, no-charge hosts will use your site's pages to post advertising banners.

Once your business is established, your website could become another source of revenue. This is especially true for merchandise vendors. Adding order forms, shopping carts and online payment options makes a website more complicated to design but imagine how nice it would be to increase your sales by a few hundred bucks a month from people ordering your products on the web.
Food vendors can develop supplemental catering businesses. What a great way to maintain an income during the offseason. A web site is vital for supporting and promoting a separate catering venture.

The next section is on social media, where I will state emphatically and repeatedly that you do not need to devote hours of your life to social media. However, you do need some kind of web presence. Having no Internet involvement at all these days is like not having an e-mail address or phone number. If a website seems more trouble than you care to take on, at least put up a Facebook page. Your business will not be perceived as legitimate if no one can find you on the Internet.

<u>Social Media</u>

Ugh, how to tackle this one. Just hearing about social media gives me the creeps. We're bombarded with reports about Facebook trends, what's happening in the "Twittersphere," who's hot on Instagram. If you are into social media, use social media; if you are not, don't. Some people swear you MUST post regularly to all social media outlets. You have to tell all your followers what you are doing and where you are going to be all the time!

Really? Do you think hundreds of Instagram followers are going to attend a festival, simply because a vendor posted a picture of their stand from the festival? Would people who aren't fans of country music attend a country music jamboree, just to visit a single vendor?

Sure, I get it, social media is fun–for folks who think social media is fun. Heck, I post pictures and videos from events to my website regularly. However, I don't expect people to come to events and visit my booth because of my website posts. My website is designed to impress event organizers and for the fun of letting friends and family see the crazy stuff, I get myself into.

If you've figured out a way to make social media marketing work for you and you like doing it, go crazy with it! If you aren't into devoting huge chunks of your life to tweeting, posting, commenting, and tagging, your business will grow fine without it.

Maintaining a social media presence is a part-time job. The five, ten, twenty hours a week you have to commit to posting updates could be much better spent on other elements of your business. That is unless you LIKE posting updates. If social media is your recreation, knock yourself out. But don't believe astonishing success will follow if you spend half your waking hours seeking followers. Every business does not have to tweet or fail. Not everyone likes social media.

Driving in a tunnel makes it hard to see other roads. People in the social media tunnel, tell us the only way to succeed is with social media. Meanwhile, only a tiny fraction of social media messages reaches the viewers. How many of the half-billion tweets posted yesterday did you read? If you could read one Tweet every five seconds and all you did was read Tweets all day every day, you would not live long enough to read all the Tweets posted yesterday. Don't get the jitters over Twitter. Likewise, don't fret over Facebook. How many of the 2.5 billion Facebook users do you follow or follow you?

Forgive me if my view on social media seems harsh. I don't despise using digital devices to connect with people and I don't scorn people who love tweeting and tagging and posting. I'm simply fed up with the worship of social media. We're told social media is the end-all, be-all marketing tool for all businesses and professions. That simply is not true.

Social media is wonderful–for people who think social media is wonderful.

Those people can use it, live their lives on it, spend half their days on it, if that's what they're into. If you love social media, you will find ways to benefit from it. If you don't love social media, don't worry; your vending business will get along fine without it.

Mobile vending is what I call a "non-relationship" business. We don't need to chase social media followers. A customer buys something from us and goes on their way. We don't know their name; we don't create a record of their purchase history and we don't need to stay in touch with them after the sale.

After you've been in business for a few years and you've done the same events several times, you will be delighted when repeat customers begin to seek you out. I beam with pride when people see my stand and tell their friends, "Oh good, Tropic Hut is here again. You have to try their Java Silkie!"

That's very satisfying but proud as it may make me feel, I'm sure no one would attend a festival solely because my Tropic Hut stand was there. It's wonderful to see repeat customers. I don't need to have them follow me online.

Relationship businesses are things like banking, real estate, advertising, and insurance. People in those businesses are perpetually networking, going to business mixers, and Chamber of Commerce functions–and desperately pursuing social media followers. They're the ones who chase followers. Did you catch the irony of that? Chasing followers?

We mobile vendors may not form relationships with our customers but we are wise to build a network of fellow vendors and event organizers. After all, to get to our customers we have to get into events. Good relations with other vendors and event organizers get us into better events.

I send Christmas Cards to the organizers of events I work each year. Fellow vendors I've become friends with are also on my Christmas Card list, as well as in my e-mail address book. In this age of political correctness, some may not be into sending Christmas Cards. In that case, send non-religious New Year greeting cards: "Looking forward to another year of great fun and successful festivals!"

If I come across something interesting or funny, I share it with my vending buddies in a group e-mail. On several occasions, fellow vendors have tipped me off to good events or recommended me to event organizers. When organizers of good festivals start inviting you to participate in their events, that's when you know you've arrived.

Note that none of my social interactions with event organizers or fellow vendors is expected to gain customers for my vending business. It's networking with event organizers so I can gain access to customers at festivals and it's socializing with others in my field but it's not intended or expected to reach customers directly. If that's how you use social media–you know, to socialize–your expectations are in the right place.

With that suggestion on networking, we come to the close of this guide. I hope you have found a few tips that help build a successful vending business. People sometimes ask what I think are the most important factors for a mobile vendor's success. I can narrow that down to three things: products, signage, and capacity to handle rushes.

CHAPTER 7

Launching and Post-Launching Tips to Keep the Food Truck Running

The launchpad is ready to release and it is time to rev up the engines and stoves of the food truck. Marketing is essential to keep any business running. You should help the business to get noticed so that you can lure in customers. Competitors in the same field of business are never going to rest and make it easier for you. You must advertise and market yourself and your food product efficiently. Here are some marketing tips for the food truck business:

<u>Set up weekly specials:</u> After the launch, you must gain speed and traffic in business. If a customer likes a specific food item like a Mexican taco, you could have "Taco Tuesdays" where you serve the customers tacos at half the

normal price. This will spread the word and will assure you a lot of crowds.

<u>Be one with the community:</u> Get close with the community you want to serve. Sponsor for a local sports event or try helping in a charity. Also, find ways to tie up with other business owners in the community.

<u>Hold contests:</u> People love contests and they are an excellent idea to promote your food truck business. Promote contests through social media and other forms of advertising.

<u>Celebrate often:</u> You do not need a big reason to celebrate. Opt for smaller holidays and make things exciting and new for the customers. Show the spirit of your celebration through the food you offer.

<u>Have an inner circle:</u> Treat your most valuable customers nicely and create an inner circle with them. Offer them discounts and earn their trust by being sweet and nice to them.

After all this, it is also important that you choose the perfect spot to put up the food truck. Make sure that you choose a place where there will be a lot of hungry people. Park your vehicle next to a commercial or industrial space. Also, make sure that there are no serious competitors around to spoil your day. When you want to choose a place, also find out about the events that might happen regularly at that place. Try to participate in such events and maximize your profit in doing so. Assure that you find out about the ease with which you can get the licenses to put up your food truck in these events. Do not feel bad to partner up. Partner up with a mall or building complex that will allow you to set up a spot on their property.

Tips to Sustain the Successful Run After Setting Up

It is essential to keep the business running in a smooth and controlled manner. This will make your brand profitable in the long run.

<u>Feel free to market yourself</u>

Marketing extends beyond the beginning phase and it is essential to keep the food truck running. Take advantage of digital media and its marketing platforms. Tweet about the places you are going to put up the stall, connect with Facebook, and maintain a Facebook page to post regular updates. Have a well-planned social media marketing scheme and try to lure in more customers by showing the merrier sides in dining with you. Also, make sure that you deliver the quality and service that you have advertised. False advertising can put a hole in the whole process.

Think freely and do not attach yourself to an idea

Even if you have found the perfect spot for business and even it had worked well for a long time, there is a possibility of dwindling of sales. Take time to re-plan and think about moving to another new area. Do not be too rigid in the way you think. It is a waste of time and you might end up losing the business in the process.

Expand on the revenue streams

Change over the course of time and try implementing new business ideas. Take risks and always be on the lookout for new opportunities. Cater to events and festivals to increase the profits you take. Get out of the comfort zone and try new and exciting things. Keep the energy and flow running.

Be open to teaming up

Do not feel bad about teaming up with other food truck owners out there. You could get a lot out of it because people who eat out of food trucks are most likely to change their trucks often. Pick a crowded place and a friendly food truck owner to club your business with. Cater to that crowded place together and get the best out of that situation. It need not be regularly but it is good to team up once in a while. People will also love the variety that you and your friend in business have to offer.

Keep networking

Make friends with people who have a strong influence over the place. Drop the prejudice and consider asking other truck owners to get valuable referrals for events and festivals. People might help you and you might even expand your network. Do not live in your world and miss out on the exposure that others have to offer to you.

Make a good investment in your staff

Make sure that you help the staff grow within their positions so that they stay trustworthy and faithful in the future. You must treat them with the respect they deserve and you must acknowledge their good work. The process of bringing in and training new staff is not only time-consuming but also costly.

<u>Put a good price tag on your food items</u>

Being new to the business doesn't mean that you have to offer food for a very cheap rate. If your food is tasty and has very good quality, feel free to charge the price that will benefit your system. It is vital to remember that people are ready to pay for the good stuff. Keep your eyes on the quality of the food you serve and you will automatically see a growth in business.

These tips and techniques are essential in your path to become a successful food truck owner. So, get out there and put out some interesting items on the menu to keep the hungry taste buds on fire. Serve with a bright smile on your face and complete love in your heart. There are a whole lot of people to feed in this world and it is high time that you realize that you can be the change you want to see. Thrive and work hard to serve the tastiest food on wheels and make sure that you touch the lives of people with what you do.

Food Safety

Food safety is a global issue, spanning several specific urban areas.

The food safety guidelines aim to prevent contamination of foods and that may cause food poisoning. It is done across various channels, some of which are:

- Sanitizing and proper cleaning of all surfaces, utensils, and equipment
- Maintaining a high standard of personal hygiene, in particular, handwashing
- Chilling, heating and storing food correctly with regards to equipment, environment, and temperature
- Introducing effective methods of pest control

- Understanding food poisoning, food intolerance, and food allergies

Regardless of the reason you are handling food, whether it's part of your profession or cooking at home, it's important to always follow the proper food health principles. There is any number of possible food hazards in a food handling environment, many of which have severe implications with them.

According to the new annual study by OzFoodNet, Tracking the Instances and Causes of Diseases Potentially Transmitted by Food in Australia, 5.4 million cases of foodborne disease occur in Australia per year which are preventable. The incidents caused by these diseases is estimated at an astounding AUD 1.2 billion.

In American food businesses when referring to food safety, ownership is placed solely on the business itself. It must ensure that all foods handled and prepared within the business are safe to eat. Many are expected to hire a qualified Food Safety Manager to help the food business fulfill this duty.

How to Get Smart About Food Safety?

If you have never worked in the food service industry you need to enroll in a program that certifies you and your employees with the necessary credentials that demonstrate your knowledge of food safety. ServSafe is the nationally recognized food code authority for the United States. They offer food safety training for food handlers and food managers that work in the restaurant industry. Many states are now requiring food service professionals to be ServSafe certified. Check with your local health department to see if this is a requirement for you.

Food Safety Resources

There are many food safeties resources out there to help educate you about proper food storage, food preparation, and food holding requirements. The bottom line is you need to be armed with the necessary information to protect the public from foodborne illnesses. Each state has different requirements but all state and city health departments develop their regulatory requirements based on the U.S. Food and Drug Administration's (FDA) Food Code. States and city health departments are permitted to add additional safety measures to their regulatory requirements to address additional safety concerns.

Here is a list of some public website resources to bookmark for future reference:

- U.S. Food and Drug Administration Public Website www.fda.gov - type in the keywords 'Food Code' on their search tool for the most current Food Code

- U.S. Department of Agriculture Public Website www.fsis.usda.gov - type in the keywords 'Food Safety Education' on their search tool for various insightful training on food safety.

- Nebraska Department of Agriculture Public Website www.nda.nebraska.gov - type in the keywords 'Focus on Food Safety' for an excellent guide on food safety

Why Must I Use Commercial Equipment?

The most common complaint I hear from new food truck operators and restaurateurs that have never worked in the food industry is "why do I have to purchase expensive commercial food equipment when the food equipment I use at home is just as good?" These aspiring entrepreneurs believe household refrigerators and freezers are sufficient to handle the day-to-day job required to operate their food establishment, not to mention household units are less expensive than commercial units.

Here is the answer to the aforementioned question: **the temperature recovery rate for refrigeration units designated for household use cannot keep up with the constant open and closing of the refrigeration doors during food truck or restaurant use.** Temperatures inside the cooling section of units for household use may exceed the safe temperature range for the food being held, resulting in bacteria growth and food safety risks passed on to the customer as foodborne illnesses.

If one of your customers gets sick due to you or your employees' failure to adhere to proper food safety, your business is done – you will be asking your old employer for your job back because you neglected to apply simple food safety procedures.

Commercial refrigeration units are not cheap and range from $1,200-$9,000 depending on the brand and the number of doors the unit is equipped with. Reach-in coolers need to be capable of keeping refrigerated foods at a temperature of 41 º F or less. Reach-in freezers need to be capable of keeping frozen foods at a temperature of 0 º F or less.

All commercial equipment used for the refrigeration, cooking, and or hot-holding of food will have a commercial-grade specification affixed to the unit. The most recognized commercial-grade standard is ANSI or NSF but some other standards also exist and are acceptable too. The bottom line, if your equipment is labeled "Household Use" it is not approved for commercial food service.

<u>Some Basics About Food Safety</u>

This part of your business is not the most glamorous part of your operation but trust me it will put you out of business if you do not take it seriously. Food safety does not require an advanced degree in Biology, just simple attention to detail. After you successfully pass the required food safety course requirements for the state where your business will operate keep a copy of the 'Focus on Food Safety' booklet, previously mentioned in the list of public website resources, on your food truck and review it with your employees monthly.

Maintaining Your Food Truck in The Winter

Half of the nation is encountering freezing cool, harsh climate during this part of the year. This is particularly noteworthy for organizations that partially or entirely rely upon climate conditions for deals. What's more, regardless of whether these businesses can discover approaches to keep deals up while they persevere through the chilly weather, they additionally need to keep up the working hardware that spends long periods of time outside.
Food trucks are no special case for this standard. Just like with vehicles, truck proprietors continually run into challenges with firing up the engine in cold conditions. Even though you and other catering truck proprietors should expect to set up your trucks before the winter season begins, if you haven't

there are still simple approaches to do maintenance jobs and safety checks that are explicit to chilled air and winter driving before the end of the season. Here are a couple of steps to guaranteeing that your mobile food stand endures through the rest of the season:

Ensure your normal upkeep is up to date

If you do this during the snowy season, you can help ensure that you don't experience unforeseen repairs.

Take a look at your antifreeze

To help protect your food vehicle, ensure that your truck contains a full degree of 50/50 blend of antifreeze and water all through the season. You can get this investigated at a service station or test it yourself with the proper device.

Check your tires

Winter isn't a simple season on your tires. On a cold highway, these are the most significant highlights among you and the guard rails. The National Highway Transportation Safety Board reports that you need at least 2/32" of profundity to be protected. What's more, check your tire strain to ensure that your altogether siphoned up-tires will, in general, not lose pressure in the cold.

Review and replace your wipers

Your wipers are even progressively susceptible to damage when you and your food trailer's group are continually utilizing them to remove ice, debris, snow, and hail from the windshield. When you are driving, you rely upon your wipers to clear anything from your vision that is laying on the exterior, so it's basic to ensure they can carry out their responsibility. In the winter it turns out to be considerably progressively essential to focus on your catering food truck's wipers as your truck will encounter sand and salt from the highway department's snow cleanup schedule.

Watch out for your windshield washer liquid

It's a tendency for vehicle proprietors to utilize an abundance of washer liquid to help melt ice from the windshield of their food trucks' in the winter. As this is the situation, ensure that you check and replace your washer liquid.

<u>Proceed with your yearly upkeep as necessary, in addition to your winter maintenance</u>

So, as to ensure that your food trailer is performing well all year, you should normally clean your battery posts, examine your spark plug wires, investigate your brakes and check your motor oil.

Complete these undertakings throughout the winter season so, your food truck and its passengers can be as prepared and safe in the cold weather as possible. Try not to let this season put you out of commission!

Successful Food Truck Marketing

<u>Food truck occasions!</u>

A food truck occasion displays an extraordinary chance to attract the interest of both new and existing purchasers. These occasions are regularly composed by somebody attempting to make a buck on collecting rents to be a part of the occasion but that is life in America. It very well may be justified, despite all the trouble but you should verify who else will be there and who is the clientele attending. You certainly don't need competition in your food. Furthermore, you would prefer not to serve your vegan cooking to a lot of rodeo types. Similarly, as with anything, thoroughly consider the cooperative energy of attending and figure if the cost to do it merits the potential return.

Different sorts of occasions might be functions of associations that need to pull in individuals to their organization or events. These undertakings offer an enormous upside since you will be connected in the client's observation with the association supporting the occasion. That can give great PR.

A key factor to the accomplishment of an occasion relies upon the coordinator's investment into appropriate advertising of the occasion, to incorporate catchy posters and fliers. Some attention ought to be paid to your food truck and the role it plays in the bigger event. Try not to be shy to demand what inclusion you and your truck will have in this advertising.

Putting resources into your very own Branding.

Here you will have the test of putting inadequate time and center to branding something that if you have no experience with it will be difficult. I propose you go with an organization that offers branding and marketing services. Branding has a gigantic upside, for it separates you from your opposition memorably and uniquely, it's classy to have your own branded items.

Your name reveals everything...

Or possibly it should try to. A name is generally critical to pass on in a short and direct fashion as possible what you are, what you do, and in case of food, what you serve. What about Sizzle Stix (a Gourmet Street's brand) that sells tasty kabob foods skewered on a stick. Get it? What about Sweeties, they serve everything for the sweet tooth. What do you think the Dog Truck sells? (I'm not proposing this, you may get a young man who wants to purchase a dog from you). But you get my point, I hope. There's the "Take the Dump Truck." Can you think about what it sells? Dumplings... I don't think so!

Ensure your truck is appealing.

It's genuinely counterproductive to spend all the cash on a new, completely equipped food truck, just to leave it standard and dull. A lovely vinyl wrap, stupendously structured is definitely worth the cash and will attract the eye of all who you drive by. Get innovative and make an external appearance that matches the alluring food you are offering inside.

Train your staff to have astounding customer service.

It ought to be your #1 priority, as the initial five seconds of cooperation between another client and your staff will either make a client or the inverse, best case scenario, the customer may leave and pass-by disinterested and even under the least favorable conditions, cause somebody to insult your truck to other people. Train your staff to smile always, be selfless and benevolent.

Qualities That A Food Truck Vendor Must Have

In the past, individuals thought of food trucks as a source of junk food. Anyway, as time passed by, the value and the functionality of food trucks have been uncovered. Individuals who are swamped at work and have no opportunity to take their lunch in the solaces of their homes or eateries rely on food truck proprietors to bring them healthy meals.

In view of the notoriety of vending trucks, few people who might need to earn are venturing to this kind of business. If you wish to be a successful food truck trader, you should have the following attitudes:

Patience

Finding a vehicle that you can transform into a vending truck involves a great deal of time. There are a lot of organizations that sell vehicles that are perfect for being converted into food trucks. If you lack the patience in scouring the market for the best deal that you can get, at that point, you might be deceived by merchants who take advantage of the high demand for vehicles. If you need to set aside cash and get the best vehicle you should be able to look for the best deal.

Innovator

A food seller should be productive. Being innovative means being to get the same number of requests as you can from the workplaces that are situated at places where your food truck will pass on. If the seller is innovative, then he will be able to convey his products to numerous workplaces and offices.

Friendly

Significantly, you can assemble affinity with your clients. This is because if they consider you to be a well-known face and a business person who considers nothing but profits. Friendliness means you will be selling a greater amount of your merchandise and items.

Creative

Clients don't care for routine food. This is the reason why they would avoid heading off to the office cafeteria to eat their meals. You should be creative in your menus. Ensure that you have an assortment of food that you can offer to your clients. It won't just satisfy your clients; however, you will likewise be able to remain in front of your competition.

<u>Time Management</u>

Manage time successfully. You should recall that the basic reason why you are starting a food truck business is for adaptability and freedom rather than simply being positioned in one location. If you can manage your time well, then you can serve numerous clients. The more places you can visit in one day, the more clients you serve, the more profits you gain.

The food truck business is anything but a difficult business to learn. If you have every one of these attributes, then you will unquestionably become wildly successful.

CHAPTER 8

False Assumptions About Owning a Small Business

When individuals decide to start a small business or any business venture, most often, they start the process with assumptions ingrained in their brains about what the business environment would be like, without truly questioning what they hear or read. Having a belief without documented proof and research to back up that belief often leads the aspiring entrepreneur to make decisions and create strategies for their business that oftentimes is completely wrong for their business and they are left wondering what happened.

Some common false assumptions and strategies are:

MYTH #1: Relying on others for answers and information blindly

Do not believe everything you read and hear. Instead, get into the habit of researching information and knowledge you obtain from others and understand WHY and **"connect the dots"** between facts and concepts. If you do not know why situations and facts are the way they are, then you will not have the ability to critically think through every situation you will come across in the life span of your business. If you have a business and you find yourself unsure of what you should be doing, why people aren't buying or you are standing there twiddling your thumbs confused, then you either have done something wrong, do not talk to your customers enough to know what they need and want or you do not know enough about your business.
There is power in the knowledge YOU have and as a business owner, you should KNOW your business and all of the influencers around it. If you have control and knowledge about every facet of your business, you will know how to handle most if not all situations that happen within your business life span.

MYTH #2: There are free grants and banks that will loan individuals money if they are starting a business

This is not true. You will need to contribute capital out of your pocket to fund your business, EVEN if you are looking for funding from other sources. Lenders, for example, will expect you to contribute at least 15-20% of your funds (sometimes more than that) into the business or they will automatically assume that you have no faith in your business idea or that you do not have any financial responsibility or know-how.

Also, there are no truly **free grants** out there that will just give anyone funding. A few grants that do exist, are usually listed on www.grants.gov . These grants are usually geared towards educational institutions, nonprofits, specialized industries, or emerging technologies within industries **for a reason**.

If you are the type of person that would not hand over your money to a random stranger just because they are starting their business, do not assume others will. This includes financial institutions also. They too are doing business. They cannot stay afloat if they approved anyone walking through their doors asking for capital.

If you haven't found any grants you qualify for yet, it is because free grants for the general public typically do not exist and/or you do not meet the required stipulations provided by grants. Also, grants are never **free,** they always have stipulations attached and/or goals & requirements you have to achieve ahead of time before they fund your business.

MYTH #3: People will automatically love and know about your business when you officially launch

This is also not true. Remember, YOUR BUSINESS is the new entity that is coming into an already established marketplace. It is up to you to grab the attention of consumers who are already buying products/services that are similar to yours, from other businesses that are already in existence and convey to them in a way that they understand and like; that your business exists and has better value for them.

This isn't a **field of dreams** where if you build a business on a random street corner or create a website on the internet, that people will automatically know who you are. There are 14+ billion websites on the planet, for instance. How do you expect them to find you right away? It takes the proper marketing strategies and channels for them to hear about you and that takes time.

The more that you do pre-grand opening/launch marketing the more time you save when you do officially open.

MYTH #4: Being resistant to the notion that your original business idea and concept will change and evolve

Everyone who wants to start a business, typically falls in love with the concept that they want to start. So much so, that they are resistant to change any facet of it. The problem is consumers will only buy from a business if that business offers something that is a solution to their problems and needs.

Having a business isn't primarily about what YOU want, it is primarily about providing what potential customers want. Their purchases are what will be responsible for what hopefully keeps you in business. If you don't focus on their needs, wants, and preferences–they will not buy from you and you will not have the revenue to pay your expenses. At that point, you will no longer be in business.

You will need to put the customers first and their preferences change all the time. That is how trends and technology changes. As trends change, the marketplace you are in will change and your original business concept will have to evolve to keep in step with your changing industry. If you do not change with it, you will be left behind and will ultimately have to shut down your business.

MYTH #5: There is one set magic formula for everyone who wants to start a business

This is not true as well. Somewhere along the way in life, aspiring entrepreneurs grew up believing that there is some magical checklist in the sky that, if followed, their business will be successful. This is destructive thinking.

Although there are basic business principles and a basic flow, the start-up process for every single business, including ones in the same industry, **will be different.** There are **no** predesigned processes or timelines for your business because every business and vision within each business is different. The proper strategies and operations for your business all depend on what YOU want your business to look like and then you apply the basic principles to that.

Following a pre-designed checklist or any checklist will not make you successful, being aware of business principles, the influencers around and in your business, and having the proper strategies for your business are the **minimum** you will need to put your business on the right path.

These are just some of the false and risky assumptions that I see aspiring entrepreneurs and current business owners have every single day. Having these risky assumptions is what makes the business owners create strategies and decisions that negatively impact a business and they are left wondering where they went wrong.

The point of the five assumptions I listed above (and there are a lot more to this list) is that as the business owner, it is your responsibility to make the right decisions for your business and you cannot be a proper business owner if you are relying on anyone other than yourself to make your business successful. You have to plan ahead of time and take the logical steps to achieve the goals you want. You have to have patience and you have to think through every situation that you encounter. You have to make time for this.

CHAPTER 9

How to Keep A Business Healthy in the Long Run

Surrounded in the least ambiguous terms, a business is a venture that gives an administration or an item to customers, in exchange for cash. Without customers, businesses would come up short. Furthermore, as an entrepreneur and proprietor of an online business, besides a reasonable pool of customers, you likewise need to have an impressive repertoire of hard and delicate aptitudes to see your business through good and bad times.

What Else Do You Need?

Times change and the components that started the seed of life for your business can change with them. Consider Kodak - the world leader in photographic film, it failed when it couldn't adjust rapidly enough to exploit the ascent of advanced imaging technology. The company reimagined itself and declared that it offered "bundling, useful printing, realistic interchanges and expert administrations for businesses around the globe," after coming up from the fiery debris of its previous success.

You need a long-term vision: where would you like to go with the business and where do you need it to take you?

What you likewise need for your business are good relationships. Strong relationships with your peers, accomplices, and partners in your business community are additionally imperative. Nobody ever really gets anywhere worth moving to, independent from anyone else. Help people, fabricate friendships, and your reward would be a supportive community, a profound feeling of belonging, and the benefit of having the option to give back.

To watch out for the health of your business, you need cozy information on what that means precisely.

What are your parameters for ideal health? In what key areas? What information do you need?
How would you track and accumulate the data you need? How far into the future would you be able to extrapolate from it?
What are your support plans in case of awful times, lean times, and crises?
What actions are you taking to forecast trends and search ahead for changes that will affect your business?

How Are You Preparing to Adjust So You Can Meet Those Trends?

There are things past your sphere of impact: what you can directly affect is the relationship you have with your customers, with your people, and with your peers. Concentrate on what you can change, construct substantial reserves to foresee and deal with the things you can't.

Customers and a flexible supporting workforce contribute directly to your bottom line and the survival of your business. Your test is to discover practical ways to enable them to be getting it done for whatever length of time that you need your business to last.

Any good business proprietor needs to be personally aware of the considerable number of things affecting the health of their business and for long term success to be assured, you are required to comprehend what you are dealing with to keep people interested in your items and relying on you. That means keeping up quality, support, and staying in contact with the need of the times.

Conceptualize gainful changes to stretch out beyond the bend. It resembles gaming in the future when you do this. Foresight as connected to industry trends and longer reaching shifts help you plan for the essential advancement of your business and avoid many changes. A piece of being successful is guaranteeing the strength of your business, which means having the option to navigate through harsh waters and make it out securely.

It's a presence of mind: to navigate well, you need to have a generally excellent idea of where the harsh patches would present themselves. If you can get a good idea where they would be simply the likeliest to give ahead of time, you can avoid them and if you can't locate some other way past them, you can prepare your business to withstand the inconvenience and the changes until you get clear.

Plan for The Most Exceedingly Terrible

Disaster planning is a piece of good business rehearses. This is where you dream up the most exceedingly terrible things that would possibly be able to happen to demolish your business and afterward, concoct ways to deal. You let your feelings of dread run wild, at that point when you have given them a chance to run down, you let rationale dominate.

Disaster-planning and prevention preparedness doesn't need to be done and completed all in a day. That would be genuinely debilitating and if you do choose to do this, enroll help from people who can offer firm support and understanding regarding what are the situations that may happen and to prompt you on those, so that you are ready to face them, when they occur.

Develop Solid Relationships

In case you missed reading between the lines, besides disaster planning, you likewise need a community of supportive, liberal people who you realize you can trust and rely on and that means developing solid, commonly gainful relationships crosswise over different social gatherings and assorted foundations. What you need to share for all intents and purposes is having the option to trust each other and respect what each brings to the table.

These sorts of relationships don't become medium-term. It requires investment and real exertion to developed stable connections, so you need to know about what you bring to the relationship and be happy to offer assistance notwithstanding when it doesn't appear to be required and prepare to finish if you don't have any desire to connect with people who take and don't give anything back, at that point, make an effort not to be one of those people. You can't get what you don't give, not in the long-term and we are talking long-term here, isn't that so?

Check-In, Assess, and Change as You Push Ahead

Set aside active squares time at regular interims to check in with your objectives, progress, and ventures. Similarly, as you can utilize every time on the weekend to plan and prepare for the week ahead, you can likewise use those times to assess the previous week and see what you can improve, adjust or drop in the week to come. Do this exercise, also for the end of the month and put those months in their place toward the end of one quarter to assess and plan forward to the next quarter.

CHAPTER 10

How Do I Create Profitable and Predictable Processes

Before you can start building your predictable processes, you need to understand:

- Why you need them?

- What results you are looking to achieve?

- Who the processes should be created for?

- Where processes should be applied?

- How they will help you, your team, and your business growth?

- When do you need to create them?

Start with collecting data on all the tasks your team works on throughout the year. Then you can start formulating a plan of attack to build the necessary systems and processes.

Don't be afraid to question everything in your business. Going through this technique to find out what needs to be streamlined will likely ruffle feathers among your team, especially if they have been a part of your organization for a long time. Remind yourself constantly why you are going through the trouble of creating processes in the first place.

Start with just one operation at a time so you don't overwhelm yourself, your team, or your customers. I use the Five Ws to discover how I can best optimize the process needed:

- **Why** is the process needed?

- **What** are the desired results?

- **Who** is involved?

- **When and Where** is the process used?

- **How** will it affect the rest of my operation?

Answering the above questions will enable you to make informed conclusions before making an informed decision.

Now write out and number each step in the current method used to accomplish the specific task. Observe the current method taking place. Keep an eye out for all the inefficiencies happening because you haven't been taking the time to ask, "Why?"

Once you have all the steps written, you should be able to see more clearly:

- How each step relates to the others?

- Which steps are unnecessary?

- Which steps can be completed together?

- How reducing steps will reduce costs and time?

- How advancing your technology could improve efficiency?

- Where adding steps could increase efficiency, quality control, and output?

Creating predictable processes is not always about conserving resources. In some cases, the increased output can be a big result of optimizing your processes by adding just a few extra steps.

Can You Franchise A Food Truck?

Most new food truck proprietors stroll into this industry with an entrepreneurial spirit, stirred due to and despite, the poor economy and all the more especially, the loss of a job. Given this downturn and despite it, we have seen a national ascent in the food truck industry.

When we think about the word 'entrepreneur', we regularly overlook that this word doesn't just imply people that have made business thoughts from scratch. Rather, entrepreneurs are business owners that have taken on types of risk that the vast majority are reluctant or incapable to effectively manage.

This definition opens up an entire course for aspiring food truck entrepreneurs to take on. Instead of making it necessary to suddenly become a brand-advertising expert, creative designer, or master chef, you may choose to turn into a food truck franchisee-which accompanies the greater part of the advantages of working in the food truck industry with less of the duty. It's ideal for people who have next to zero business foundation.

Let's take a look at a rundown of the pros and cons of joining a franchise:

Pros:

- There are fewer forthcoming decisions. Within a franchise, you are given instant brand acknowledgment. The menu, the name, and the design are given to you.

- You will have the expert help you need. The corporate office will provide you with help and staff that can address concerns and questions. This can be particularly useful for new business owners in the mobile food industry, as they may be new to how to manage issues that emerge.

- You have a name. What's more, with that name comes business. Your name is as of now known all through the city, state, and, sometimes, even the entire country.

Cons:

- Food truck franchisees need capital and loads of it. These endeavors can run up to $500,000 just to join them. What's more commonly that this price tag goes against the reason that business owners are looking to go into this industry in any case. All things considered, opening up a food truck should be a lot less expensive than running a physical café, right?

- The idea of the truck–name, design, and menu are given to you. Similarly, as this fills in as a pro for joining a franchise, it can likewise be viewed as a con. It takes into consideration little innovativeness, which is the thing that most business visionaries thrive on.

- You are paying royalties and other fees (relentless).

So, what will you choose? Keep up a receptive outlook and settle on key choices that are in line with your desires and personality. Opening any food truck business, regardless of whether it's a franchise or a truck from scratch is a long-haul choice that shouldn't be trifled with.

CHAPTER 11

Food Truck Business Success Tips

Get Creative with Your Sauces

If you don't plan on serving foods that involve the traditional mustards and ketchup, you can ignore this one. However, for those of you who do, it's a good idea to put an extra effort into the staples to make them a bit more exciting.

Building on the example above, we used "double-smoked ketchup" and "ballpark mustard." The best way to follow through on these claims is to have a slightly more exciting ketchup or mustard. It doesn't take much effort to spruce these up a bit, and if you can add a bit of extra flavor to these, people will remember you for it.

Unless you are already familiar with how to do it, go online and check out how to make a good mayonnaise, or how to make your ketchup and mustard a bit more exciting. For my truck, we would mix a certain BBQ sauce with the ketchup, as well as something a bit spicy to make it a better tasting and more exciting ketchup. Mustard is great because there are so many different types of mustard that people rarely try. If you are not into making your own, check out what else is out there. A lot of people are in the dark when it comes to exotic mustard, and you can use this to your advantage by using a type they have never seen before.

*On a side note, it is still a good idea to have the classics there, as some people aren't interested in trying something new, and would prefer to stick with what they know.

As the weeks go by and you have more street days under your belt, you will want to keep track of how you are doing, so let's look at how best to do that…

Plan the Work, Work the Plan

Owning a food truck business can be a standout amongst the most agreeable of all businesses in the world. Consider it! Bolstering hungry individuals delicious, crisply cooked, heavenly suppers at costs you'd pay at the neighborhood greasy spoon. Be that as it may, before getting into this business, you must do some planning and thinking to make sense of, if you have the stuff to be successful. As with getting into any business, numerous components need to be considered. At the base of every one of these contemplations is the issue: "Would you say you are ready to work for yourself?"

You will be forceful, straightforward, and arranged to work your plan carefully before you can like to make progress. More food trucks are hitting the lanes regularly, and it must be your primary goal to guarantee your place among them and eventually ascend over the competition.

First, find out who and where the competition is? Make a rundown of the considerable number of cooking styles and choose what you can serve that will be unique and generally welcomed in your commercial center.

Everything from your logo, truck structure to your decision on what to cook, in short, everything about your business must be unique. Of course, you will be sorted out when you are well organized, cognizant, and eco inviting. Investigate to some degree every day, regardless of whether this situation energizes you or alarms you half to death, this may decide if you are up to be a gourmet food truck owner/administrator or not.

At 5:00 a.m., rise and sparkle. In a couple of hours, most of the world will be awake and every one of them hungry. You need to plan to bolster them.

At 5:30 a.m., stock up at the supermarket for crisp fixings (this could have been done the previous night if you have a POS framework).

At 6:00 a.m., drive to your assigned prep-kitchen, where you will meet your staff, and start getting ready food for the truck. For instance, cutting vegetables, apportioning the dish divides, preparing your extraordinary sauces, and so on.

At 8:30 a.m. till night (or at whatever point you make your dollar objective): serve that tasty food off your truck.

At 10:00 p.m., clean up and prepare for another group buster day tomorrow.

You will need some food information, imagination, media aptitudes, and showcasing abilities, except if you go with one of the establishment food truck organizations around. Complete a search for 'food truck establishments'. Perseverance is the name of the game. You need to be sharp when leading your research alone on the food truck business, as there are numerous guidelines relating to food trucks that contrast dependence on every city. Check with the regional branch of your nearby specialist for its specific instructions.

Trucks are mechanical, so you will need to line up a dependable and responsive repairer. This is very important. Concerning the appliances that accompany your truck, it is not a smart thought to purchase utilized, for you will never know how the past owner thought about the same thing. When they are new, these appliances are secured under their producers' guarantees. When you have purchased utilized appliances like a refrigerator, stovetop, and grill, they will by all means require an up-keep.

Concerning the bookkeeping, contracting a bookkeeper to deal with your business might be somewhat ridiculously cost shrewd, so consider somebody who knows QuickBooks or some other bookkeeping software programs. An attorney might be essential to work out the grant and stopping license, once more, there might be administrations out there that could help with this. You can also complete a search on Google.

Promoting? Indeed, this is very important. I feel compelled to press on the significance of web-based social networking as much as possible. No food truck has ever been successful without contacting the general society. The most prosperous food trucks use versatile applications, Twitter, and Facebook, among others. Keep in contact with clients, keep them near you as much as could be expected because this is another key to a successful business. Furthermore, if you need your client to know where you will be, complete a search on Food Truck versatile applications and see what's out there!

Not all food trucks owners maintain their full business time. A few trucks work just at the end of the week or after work hours. Full-time tasks, in the right area, will round up more money, yet on the other side; it requires a lot of effort. Whichever way you pick dependably keep a week after week schedule with set occasions for dealing with bills, covering government expenses, and of course for spreading the expression of your business online and among companions.

In the wake of mulling over and settling on a course of activity for your truck, record it, make a business plan that will enable you to accomplish your objectives quicker, and all the more proficiently. What's more, a reasonable business plan is essential if you need to request loans from companions or the bank. Here as well, if you need loans, search online for Food Truck SBA loans. Everybody needs to see that their money is heading off to a possible money-production attempt, so the more exhaustive you are in setting up this business; the more successful you will be in persuading others to help.

Tracking Your Progress

Keep Track of What You Sell

It will be important that for the many days you spend at a certain spot or event, a track of what you have been selling has to be kept. This means keeping track of how many of each of the items were sold. This is important for several reasons.

For one, it lets you see what food items are selling best. If you regularly keep track of everything that has sold, you will probably begin to notice that some things sell very well each week, while others seem to be lagging. Keeping track of this also lets you know if prices should be changed, either to raise them or lower them.

This may seem obvious, but it is often easy to overlook. As the person coming up with the ideas and putting together the food for sale, it's often easy for judgment to be clouded.

You will probably be thinking that everything you are selling is a bestseller because you made it and it tastes good to you. But everyone is different, and asides from a few items, it is not always easy to predict just what people will like. So, do yourself a favor and keep track of the orders.

I generally do this by writing down on each order sheet what was ordered and for how much (along with the customer's name). I then save all of these slips of paper and review them after the day is done.

You don't need to get fancy and enter them into a spreadsheet. Just write down somewhere, how much of each item was sold, so that you can compare it to future service days to identify any trends in customer orders.

Keep Track of Your Costs

Selling food on the street can be more expensive than people realize. In addition to spending long hours prepping the food and making sure everything is set up for your street service day, you will be spending a fair amount of money on all the food, not to mention gas for your truck, a potential fee for the spot, etc. Costs can build up quickly even before you start selling.

A lot also depends on what type of day it is. If it's cold or raining, you could make a lot less than you originally expected, and a lot of that food could be wasted. Though these are the costs of operating a food truck, it will be important to keep track of these costs regularly. It's very easy, particularly if you are not very keen on the business side of things, to forget about expenses and pursue your goal of making amazing food recipes for people.

This is indeed crucial, but you don't want to go broke before you realize this dream. So, whether it's every service day, every week, or whatever you think is best, you should make sure to keep track of all your expenses regularly. There's nothing worse than looking at all your bills and costs after 6 months and realizing you lost a sizable amount of money.

Try to avoid this by monitoring costs regularly. This is most notable with the actual food. You may buy enough for a big crowd, only to get rained out and be left with a lot of food that goes into the garbage.

While no one can control the weather, you can plan for bad scenarios, so before you run off to buy 30 pounds of beef, consider the spot you will be serving at, how you've done in the past, and what problems might lead you to lose money. If in doubt, it's much more cost-efficient on the side of to purchase little food and sell-out, then be stuck with mountains of wasted food that cost you more than you can afford.

Keep Track of the Day's Revenue

This is worth mentioning for those who may forget to do so. You will want to make sure that you know your total sales for each day on the street. This will be important in deciding if your menu is on point, if the spot is worth it, and if you are advertising effectively. At the end of the day, the one thing that matters is how much money you are taking home after all expenses, and the best way to keep track of this is to track your sales day by day.

This way, you can match it against costs and see if you need to make a change or if what you are doing and where you are going seems to be working. It is an easy task and one that only requires a little bit of counting before and after.

Whatever bills and coins you bring, (and you should make sure you have enough) just keep track of the total you showed up with. At the end of the day, count the total amount of money, and subtract this initial amount, and you have your total sales. The other way to do it is to take your order slips with all the orders on it and add up the total from that. That will involve writing down a price on each order slip while you are taking the orders, but this is easy to remember once you do it a few times.

Take as Many Pictures as Possible

It's easy to forget to do this in the middle of a busy day, but this is exactly the time that you should be taking lots of pictures of people receiving food, people ordering, and above all lots of traffic around your truck. These are pictures you will use later for your website and social media accounts, and you want them to be full of customers.

Taking pictures of the truck is always cool because food trucks are cool. However, what drags people in is popularity. Nearly every street service day I've done, the truck that has the most people around it is the truck that makes the most money. This isn't necessarily just due to people hanging around out in front of the truck, but it does have a big influence on people who are unsure of what to get.

When people show up to eat and they have no prior knowledge of which trucks are good and which are average, they'll often go with the crowd and choose the one with the most people out front. When your truck gets busy, you will want to sneak out if possible and take some pictures. Taking pictures from outside where everyone is lined up and waiting is perfect.

The more people hanging about your truck, the more people will be drawn to it, and the more attention and hype you will get on social media. If people see pictures of a busy truck, they'll want to try it for themselves next time they can, so be sure to make a note of this, as it is easy to forget, and these opportunities don't come around often. Take advantage of the busy hours.

Have Pictures of Your Food Visible

If you have a high-quality camera, that's good for you but it's not essential. What you will want to do is have a blown-up picture of what you are serving somewhere close to where the description of the food on the menu is.

Make sure you've brought some tape. If you don't already have a picture of the food, you are serving that day then you will want to make up an order and take a picture of it, something you should do anyway. Print this off, make sure it's big enough, and take it with you.

Not every item is completely necessary, but your main items are important, and giving people a look at them, can go a long way to getting them to buy your food.

Make it a habit of taking a picture of every item you make. It's always a good idea to have a couple of different pictures of each item, or you will discover that you end up continually using the same picture on the same social media accounts, which is not very exciting.

In addition to these pictures, once you've made food for the day, take a picture of it and post it. That is exactly what people would expect to find that day at your truck. Along with a good description, this will be sure to attract lots of customers. The sky is indeed your limit, so post as many pictures as you feel like, but be sure to get pictures of all the items you will be serving up, on social media.

This is where it's important to have older pictures, as you might not have time to take a picture of each item on the day you are serving. Newer pictures are better but it's important just to have some pictures at hand so that you can quickly throw them up on your social media platforms if you don't have time to make up an order for picture purposes.

On a side note, when you are posting these pictures, don't bother putting how much it will cost. This may put some people off before they even get there. Instead, let them see what's being offered. Hopefully, this will draw them to your truck and by the time they've ordered, a couple of extra bucks won't matter to them as much anymore.

<u>Let People Know Your Location</u>

People need to know where to find you when you are out on the street. Since you are continually on the move, many people may not know your location. This is where you should be using social media to your advantage. Once you know your schedule for the week and where you will be, get it out on social media so that people will know what days you will be on the street and where you will be.

That way, people who like your food and want to have more of it will know well in advance where they can find you. It also means that people who like the food truck scene and want to try them out will know where they can find you. This will help bring in more people on the day of selling and will mean you won't just be relying on people walking by.

It is a good idea to constantly be updating this and reminding people where you will be. Doing it early in the week is a good idea, and it's also a good idea to do it periodically throughout the week. Make sure to do it the day before you head out. That way, people will have multiple chances to see where you are and will be reminded of it throughout the week and remember when you will be at a spot near them.

Prep as Much as Possible Before Arriving

There's nothing worse than seeing people showing up at your truck window ready to order food and you are still busy chopping onions. Some things may seem like they can be done in a little time that you will be able to squeeze a few of the smaller prep jobs in, before opening, but in almost all cases you will find out that you are pressed for time once you arrive.

It always takes a bit longer to set up than you think it will once you arrive, and adding on additional prep work that could be done before arriving isn't something that should be taking up this valuable time.

Arriving there early is important but do yourself a favor and take care of the smaller prep jobs before you arrive. That way, you can focus on what needs to be done at the service spot, as well as being able to relax before starting your cooking day.
Also, just because you may be opening at noon, people will often look to show up early to avoid any potential lines and you want to be ready to take their orders, especially if other trucks are still getting ready to open.

So be prepared, prep before you arrive, and take advantage of being open before the other trucks.

Test Your Food Before You Sell It

This is probably something you are already doing anyway, but if not it's an important step to remember, for a few reasons. No matter how many times you've made the item you will be selling, when it comes to the food you can never be certain how things will turn out. It could be that something is off with the meat or cheese, or that a certain sauce doesn't taste right.

In any event, it will be disastrous if you are serving food that isn't what you thought it would be, and bad food equals unhappy customers and no repeat business. So be sure to make a few test items either the night before or the day of your event or street service.

This also gives you the chance to take a picture and put it on Instagram and Twitter, with the bonus of you getting to eat and enjoying the fruits of your labor!

Have a Tip Jar

This often goes overlooked, but it shouldn't. Having a tip jar is an easy way to get a bit of extra cash out of the gig. As you will be serving on the street, and likely only taking cash, customers will generally have some extra change, either on hand or from the change you give them when they break a bill.

And, more so than a restaurant, people are generous with tips, it just seems to be a street thing. So be sure to have a tip jar out by the window. It's an easy way to earn some extra money, and people like giving tips, it makes it a good way to connect with your customer base. If your food is great, the next time they come back, they'll be even more willing to drop a few bucks in.
Just as a tip (bad pun), I'd recommend throwing a few bucks in at the beginning of the day. This makes it appear that people DO give tips, but it doesn't make it seem like you are cleaning up. Throw something funny or interesting like a quote on the outside of the jar so that it gets noticed.

Clean the Truck at The Day's End

This is one of those things that should be obvious, and indeed is a no-brainer for a lot of people, but for people like me, it is often something that requires a little more self-discipline than I usually have at the end of a long day. Let's face it, you've been up since the crack of dawn prepping and making sure everything is ready for the day. You've been on your feet all day cooking and serving food, and finally, you are driving that big, slow truck all the way home.

Ignoring this first chance to clean can be costly. For one, you can forget, and be ready to pull out for your next service only to find the truck a complete mess and not ready to use. It can also mean that food spills can harden, and the grill and other tabletops can be a mess.

This can also lead to flies and other unwanted parties happening in your truck, which can be a real headache to clean up, especially when the food is old and rotting. Do yourself a favor and clean the truck before you finally relax.

Conclusion

Lunch trucks have been in use for over 2 decades. The fundamental thought of the lunch truck is to serve food to individuals situated in various areas.

The main lunch truck was invented way back in the nineteenth century for the military which served food to their officers. This was known as a mobile lunch service. They were served with coffee and snacks which were easy to make with the technology they had during their time. Presently, as technology has progressed and given us various equipment for kitchen use, the advanced lunch trucks carry all the vital and current amenities that are required in the kitchen.

Lunch trucks are known for their benefits. When contrasted and the stationary cafés, lunch trucks have indicated great profit and a great client base. If you can give the clients the great quality of food that they can afford, you can likewise expect a few loyal clients following in various areas that you intend to go around. As you would be moving from one spot to the others, you have the chance to serve more individuals and with various menu choices.

The underlying investment that you would make is on the vehicle. With numerous models accessible in the market, you should pick the one which will fill your need. Next would be the equipment that you require, for example, the stainless-steel sinks, oven, fridge, and other embellishments, for example, the cutlery sets, plates, and so forth before you start off with your new business, there are scarcely any rules that you need to follow. With the government presenting stringent guidelines for mobile food services, it is fundamental for you to keep every one of the principles to remain in the business.

You are likewise required to get the mobile food service permit from the legislature before kicking-off your business. You can go to the local government authorities who will help you with respect to the license details. The modern lunch trucks are furnished with current sterile solutions to keeping the environment and the earth clean; giving a hygienic atmosphere for the clients to eat their food.

If you can't invest in the underlying amount that is required for obtaining the vehicle and also the important embellishments for the kitchen, you can then approach a franchise from where you can purchase his food items. When you secure a deal with a franchise, they will give all of you the important equipment for the kitchen and the lunch truck. The main thing that you have to do is to head to various areas and serve the food. Regardless of the path you pick, mobile food service permit is a must.

If you might want to expand the benefits to the following level, present additional services that will satisfy the clients and at the same time increases the client base as well as the loyal customer following. Aside from the lunch boxes that you provide, you can likewise present ice creams and desserts on the menu.

The food truck business, though, is not a smooth sail for everyone. There are going to be a number of hurdles in your business encounters that I did not cover in this book. I've tried to cover all the fundamentals but naturally, I can't prepare you for everything. All I hope is, every now and then as you build your business, you think to yourself, "Hey, that was a good idea!" from something you read in this book.

May your difficulties be few and sales are many!